inside

inside

Australian Interiors Janne Faulkner

Photography by Earl Carter

A Sue Hines Book

Allen & Unwin

First published in 1997

A Sue Hines Book
Allen & Unwin Pty Ltd
9 Atchison Street, St Leonards, NSW 2065 Australia
Phone: (61 2) 9901 4088
Fax: (61 2) 9906 2218
E-mail: 100252.103@compuserve.com

National Library of Australia
Cataloguing-in-Publication data:

Faulkner, Janne.
        Inside: Australian interiors.
        ISBN 1 86448 346 6.
        1. Interior decoration. 2. Interior decoration –
        Pictorial works. I. Carter, Earl. II. Title.
729

Designed and typeset by Guy Mirabella
Boards photograph courtesy Max Robinson
Additional photography by Neil Lorimer, Peter Clarke,
Rodney Weidland and Richard Woldendorp
Printed in Hong Kong by South China Printing

10 9 8 7 6 5 4 3 2 1

Acknowledgements

I would like to thank, in particular, David Yencken, the late
John Ridge, Graeme Gunn, Daryl Jackson and Philip Cox,
who were so supportive when I was starting out.

My family, for their constant support and encouragement.

Our clients, who have generously opened their doors and
allowed us to photograph the interiors.

The designers and staff who have given so unstintingly to
Nexus over the years.

Laminex Industries, for their support of this book.

Rae Ganim, textile designer.

Harley Anstee, Earl Carter, Guy Mirabella, Foong Ling Kong
and Sue Hines for their help with making this book.

In memory of my mother, Mary Maslin, who said when I was six,
'If you can make your bed well, you can do anything well.'

In admiration of Harley Anstee, friend and partner in Nexus Designs.

Contents

Foreword

INSIDE IS AN APT TITLE for this book. It not only shows the principles of good design, it also demonstrates the 'inside' of Janne Faulkner's philosophy and approach.

Interiors are the most changeable elements of the built environment. Architecture is a solid statement of form and space, whereas interiors have greater flexibility and ability for inhabitants to model or amend space and therefore personalise it.

Janne Faulkner always takes the personality of her clients into account. She has a simple and direct philosophy that allows the freedom of the individual. This is done through colour, choice of fabric, furniture, paintings and sculpture. The unique combination is done with flair and intellect. Beautiful interiors are the result.

Janne is foremost an Australian; she loves the Australian landscape. She delights in its ever-changing colours from deserts to rainforest. She revels in the form of the landscape, the soft eroded forms of rock, the curved line resulting from a wave washing on the sand, or the patterns created by clouds waving across a desert landscape.

She is an advocate and patron of Australian art, particularly experimental and abstracted work, that evokes the breadth of the continent itself.

Inside is not exclusive to contemporary forms. It charmingly describes how the old and the new combine, and how the bright colours can live with the faded, and shadow and light merge to give new combination and meaning.

For those who are confused about the culture of Australia, this book gives an insight into aspects of Australian design by integrating craft, art, architecture and design into a meaningful whole.

From this philosophy, new and exciting Australian environments are created, giving opportunities for personalisation and identification. It is the first book on interiors to identify an Australian approach.

Philip Cox AO

Introduction

SOME MONTHS AGO, I visited an isolated part of the coast of East Africa while on vacation. I stayed in a simple thatched hut right on the edge of the beach, the only form of accommodation available. The entire hut was woven in sisal by villagers, and the sisal flooring was laid directly onto the sand. The walls were made in the same way as the floors, and openings in the woven body of the hut were used as doors and windows. At night, sisal panels were rolled down over the openings, turning the hut into an enveloping cocoon.

Simple cane chairs, hammocks, and a large bed of local timber made up the furnishings. At night, a mosquito net bordered with a vivid turquoise cotton formed a canopy over the bed. The splash of brilliant colour transformed the room, giving it surprise and sophistication, and lifted the interior to a whole new dimension.

The way this hut was built and furnished sums up my approach to design. It sits easily and unobtrusively in its natural setting, perfectly attuned to its environment. The materials are natural to the area and consistently used. Colour is applied with restraint, and all the more effective for the excitement and joyousness it evokes.

My basic design philosophy has remained unchanged for over thirty years, since the day I started Nexus Designs. Briefly stated, it is that the best design depends on a few fundamental principles. We look long and hard at the cultural aesthetic of the place, its space, and the framework within which we are operating. Simplicity is paramount, and more and more, I have come to believe in restraint, in paring back. At Nexus, we prefer to use a small number of materials throughout a house. Fine detailing and judicious application of colour are used to provide emphasis, surprise and excitement. Wherever possible, we rely on natural materials and finishes.

The Australia we started out in thirty years ago was a very different place; it was exciting to be offered so much opportunity and scope. We had the chance to work closely with talented designers and people who were committed to transforming the design of residential communities. From the very beginning, we were involved in projects that integrated inspired site planning, house design, landscape architecture, interior design and graphic design. The integration of all the elements and components that go into making a house has remained a cornerstone of my design philosophy.

While these basic principles have remained unchanged, other influences have crept into my design. Living in Australia, I have become increasingly aware of the extraordinary beauty of the landscape and the powerful influence it has on our lives. Increasingly, I have sought in my designs to find a unique quality that reflects the vastness and grandeur, and contrasting delicacies and subtleties, of the landscape; one that also encapsulates the special temper of Australian society, especially its freedom and casualness. In all of our commissions at Nexus, we apply colours that are drawn from the diverse landscape, both rural and urban. The rocks and soils, vegetation and wildlife, and the intensity and character of Australian light are unlike those found in any other place in the world. Using palettes based on these elements makes our work recognisably Australian.

As a designer, I am conscious of the changes taking place around the world and the role that design plays in our contemporary society. Travel and new forms of communication have increased our exposure to design from all over the world. Globalisation has made it possible for us to buy products designed by the best international designers. At the same time, the pace of change and the influence of the world-wide economy can give the sense that much of what is happening is quite outside the control of individuals. This can cause much anxiety and uncertainty. This is where design plays a role. Simple colours and textiles, particularly those that are drawn from, and echo, familiar environments help to give us a sense of security and an emotional anchoring. Today, we have at our disposal the old, the new, the familiar and the best from our own society and also from other societies with which to create our very special environment. I have come to increasingly value the contribution artists can make. Artworks such as painting, sculpture and ceramics add stimulation, give pleasure and a form of challenge and education no book or television set can provide.

Inside is about how to develop a strong, coherent and sustained design approach. Everything, from the front door to the last hook and nail, needs to be integrated and finished properly for a design to succeed. In other books you will find wonderful examples of outstanding designs and products that you can copy or acquire. But copying, dipping into this book or that magazine, selecting this piece and that piece without real reflection and a well-considered overall plan doesn't always come off. For a design to flourish, it has to reflect your needs, your cultural and social setting—you. It also has to respond to other deeper

2

feelings we all have about our familiar surroundings and all of the colours, smells, shapes, sounds and tactile qualities that evoke where we live.

The interior of any house must belong completely to the people who live in it. It should not be unduly affected by the latest fashions nor by the opinions of friends or neighbours. Successful interior design should add to your joy of living and the making of it should itself be a joyous task. It asks of you that you look deeply into yourself and have fun.

Although I have moved in many design realms and been faced with many different design issues, I have never lost my early excitement with the design of houses and their surroundings and interiors. A few weeks ago, a client came back after twenty years, wanting me to develop a new inner-city house for him. My task involved all the steps from the choice of the architect through to the completion of the interior. He asked me to visit his existing house to help him choose the pieces of furniture he should keep.

Walking into his house was like coming home. A general air of culture and fine living pervaded the atmosphere. The kitchen smelt of good cooking and fresh food. The furniture, which we had chosen all those years ago, was still suitable and durable, and would probably last another twenty years. There were good rugs on the polished floorboards. The main bedroom was simply furnished; the bed covered with white cotton sheets and doona. The collection of artwork, although highly personal, looked challenging. The lighting worked and had barely dated.

I can't wait to get to work!

Inside looks at seven thematic interiors from the city to the surf, each of which required distinctive treatment. As you go thorough each interior, you'll get an idea of the way we have interpreted the owners' needs; why, for example, a beach house on a promontory is handled differently from a suburban townhouse, or how we related the colour palette to the landscape of a lake. You'll see how we worked with the architecture of the buildings and balanced the materials we used so that the inside and outside complemented each other.

In our work at Nexus we start with a shell—a neutral background or a bare canvas—the walls, floors and ceiling of each room in the house. Furniture, textiles and artworks are used to provide colour and to add interest. Such an approach is simple, but the result is a well designed house that is a continuing joy to live in.

the houses

the town

a successful

relies on t

of unnecessa

interior

elimination

house

elements

WHAT A STOREHOUSE OF SURPRISES this townhouse, an ornate Italianate villa, is! Situated in a shady street of an inner-city suburb among blocks of flats and terrace houses, it is a successful blend of contrasts—the formal with the casual, the old with the new, the decorative with the functional. The outcome is elegant, practical and very habitable.

The house once had a rich accumulation of architectural features typical of its era: a narrow frontage, set close to the street; a fenestration and central front door that led into a central passage; two rooms on either side—sleeping on one, sitting and dining on the other; some add-ons for the kitchen and bathroom; and a small enclosed backyard for the clothesline.

Upon entering the townhouse, the visitor encounters a minimalist interior that is in sharp contrast to the flamboyant façade. The dominant feeling is of airiness and spaciousness usually associated with larger houses. The soft flowing colours of the palest yellow and grey used throughout exude warmth.

The owners regard the kitchen as the hub of the house, a place where people like to gather, so the result is a house that is slightly back to front. The kitchen is now located where one would normally expect a bedroom or sitting room. Divided only by a bank of cupboards from the narrow hall, it looks into several rooms and the courtyard, besides being an open and welcoming sight from the front door.

From almost anywhere in the house, it is possible to see through and into other areas, including the courtyard, but there is a sense that each space exists as part of the whole without surrendering its function. Several rooms have been turned into one, walls have been removed and extended, and there is little definition between the kitchen, dining and sitting rooms.

The owners chose this villa particularly for the northern aspect of the potential courtyard and extended the house on the southern and eastern sides to form a U-shaped configuration, built to the edge of the property to make the best use of the space.

The long plain wall of the house next door forms a border for the courtyard. Winter sun floods in here and into the adjoining rooms, essential when living in a temperate climate.

The courtyard acts as another room and is particularly suited for summer living and entertaining. The canvas sails hung overhead on wire guides provide shade and create interesting lighting effects.

FOLLOWING PAGES *The kitchen shelving is based on a module that is also used in the sitting room*   11
as bookcases. Cream terrazzo is used for the benchtops. The colours of the painting by Colin Lanceley
are enhanced by colourful kitchen dishes.

PREVIOUS PAGE *The early French dining table, made of fruit wood, complements the Gio Ponti chairs, which were designed in 1957. Light as a feather, they are durable and very comfortable. Storage requirements have been met with the installation of floor-to-ceiling cupboards.* ABOVE *Courtyard plantings have been chosen for their soft tones of silver, mauve and green. Two shaped weeping pears* (Pyrus salicifolia) *are the colour of sage, and the darker leaves of* Mulenbeckia *cover tall rectangular frames that moderate the glare from the high-key surfaces. A wisteria has been trained on one wall, and the garden seating has been planted with box and convolvulus.*

ABOVE *Only three main materials have been used throughout the house. Pale cream terrazzo that has been mixed and coloured with a much finer marble chip than the usual 'salami' terrazzo has been used for all the interior and exterior floors, built-in benchtops and fixed panelling.* OPPOSITE *Ornate Italianate cornices dictated the simplicity of the bedroom finishes. The windows are left uncovered except for the two that face the street. The cream-on-cream palette is the perfect backdrop for the owners' collection of richly coloured rugs, paintings, ceramics and furniture.* OVERLEAF *A Regency dining table and Hepplewhite chairs have been placed in front of a terrazzo servery. The original watercolours of Australian shipping have been framed in bird's eye maple. In the foreground is a Taacia lamp by Castiglioni.*

Many renovations start off with four good rooms. In this townhouse, there were decorative period features such as cornices, ceilings and fireplaces. It takes a degree of courage for a designer to dispose of such treasures, and to do so with the confidence that accusations of iconoclasm will not be made. Retaining them all, however, can restrict the potential for re-dedicating rooms to purposes more suited to a modern lifestyle.

Some of the beautiful original ceilings were retained. Those that were in poorer condition or may have prevented the reformation of rooms were dispensed with. The family room and kitchen, which in a previous life was a formal dining room, are crowned with their original ornate plaster cornices.

Added were a long L-shaped room that combined the formal dining room and a comfortable sitting area, and a bedroom with a connecting well-lit dressing room and bathroom.

The success of the interior relies on the elimination of extraneous elements. Attention has been given to functional aspects of living in a small open-plan house. Narrow hydronic heating panels were recessed to save space, fitted cupboards were hidden behind grey walls, and long terrazzo benchtops reduced the need for space-hungry furniture. Lighting was kept simple: the hall, sitting and dining rooms, main bedroom and bathrooms have modern flush ceilings with recessed low-voltage lighting.

23

The owner's collection of artwork formed an integral part of the interior design. Two specially commissioned works, integrated from the planning stage of the renovation, provide a focal point in the otherwise formal courtyard.

A modern sculpture in bronze and copper stands in sharp relief against the courtyard wall. A ceramic mosaic adds a whimsical element to the pond.

PREVIOUS PAGE *A wall was removed to create this L-shaped space, now the combined sitting and dining rooms.* ABOVE LEFT *The Pucci upholstery fabric comes from a private mill in Florence. Its faded gelati colours are picked up in the Iranian kilim.* ABOVE RIGHT *A gridded floor-to-ceiling shelving holds books and treasured objects.*

ABOVE *Something old and something new: a Regency side chair with tapestry seating inspired by Braque paintings alongside a leather-covered Sinbad chair.* OVERLEAF *The main bedroom opens onto the courtyard. The bed is simply dressed with crisp cream cotton sheets and doona. The paintings and rug provide little inflections of colour. The combination of diverse patterns and textures adds interest.*

the townhouse

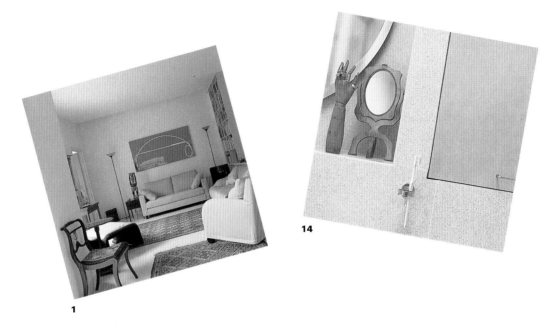

14

1

1 Before starting work, look at the spaces available and think about the way you like to live. Some walls may have to be removed, and the position of rooms looked at in light of your needs. You may require an architect or designer to assist with the structural nature of the renovation. **2** The relation between interior and exterior colour is important. In this case, the owners have chosen a colour that is sympathetic to the streetscape and the neighbouring environment. They have used a toned-down version of the exterior colour inside. **3** Spaces appear larger if wall and floor finishes are of similar colouring. (If this principle is extended through to the exterior, the courtyard feels like another room of the house.) **4** Rather than vary tiles, granite, marble or laminates in different areas, maintain the continuity of a single finish throughout. This townhouse uses terrazzo for floors, kitchen benchtops, the sideboard bench, and even the bath surrounds. **5** Furniture layout plans for all rooms are useful, especially when planning for lighting needs. Downlights are usually sufficient for small spaces, supplemented with the use of occasional lamps and uplights for mood and effect. Pendant fittings tend to break up the space. **6** The choice of kitchen benchtop materials depends on whether you are a careful or carefree cook. Stainless steel, granite and laminate are the most stain proof. Timbers and marble look good but require more care. **7** When choosing appliances, try to keep the finishes and colour the same. Do your homework on kitchen appliances. The most expensive items are not always the best, and local products are easier to service and cheaper to purchase. Modern cooktops are more versatile and have burners for woks

do it yourself

3

4

11

and fish steamers. Combinations of gas and electric hot plates provide for flexible cooking. **8** Treat windows in a simple way to control light and privacy. If you have no privacy problems, leave them bare. Otherwise, slimline blinds, architectural roman blinds in sheer linen, timber venetian shutters and curtains in natural materials that blend with the colour of the walls will ensure privacy while maintaining the continuity of space. **9** Select tiles of the same size for floors and walls in the bathroom. A pedestal basin works well in conjunction with a trolley if you do not want to use a traditional built-in vanity unit. **10** Choose upholstery fabrics that will age and wear well. Think of larger pieces of furniture as part of the shell, and use individual pieces for colour accents. **11** Consider and write down all your storage requirements. You'll need to consider how you live, the effect you'd like to create, and if you need to keep things away behind cupboard doors. **12** Privacy and security are important in townhouses. Ensure there is adequate lighting at the front entrance. **13** Once the basic finishes are selected, you have a defined shell to start on the next round of decisions. Practicality and simplicity are of the essence. Consider them when selecting wall and floor finishes, and when choosing bathroom and sanitary ware; door furniture; cupboard handles/drawer pulls; bathroom towel rails and accessories; tapware; and electrical switch plates and power points. **14** Personalise the space with your favourite objects.

a special

deserves s

the lake

treatm

landscape

house

AS REFUGES FROM THE CITY GO, this settler's cottage is different. It was originally built low down on the hillside and remained there until the lake was developed over sixty years ago. Though artificial, the lake is on a grand scale, with surrounding virgin bush that attracts wonderful bird life. One winter, with water lapping at the door, a bullock team started to move the house to the top of the hill. Under the extreme conditions, the team became bogged under the load and dropped the house. It has remained on the same site ever since, a little beyond the water's edge, but dry!

The mystic quality and the changing patterns of the water influenced the selection of colours and textures throughout the house. The original timber building turned in on itself, ignoring the magnificent outlook. The aim of the refurbishment was to maintain the house's existing charm and internal qualities, while opening up the rooms to the sumptuous view of the lake.

Today, the building has a warm and inviting quality. Its success lies in the consistent mix of gentle colours and textures. The colours of the lake and surrounding countryside determined the palette of soft greys, pale blues and creams. Old dado-height tongue-and-groove wooden boards were left in their original colour of palest blue, and a new cream colour painted above for contrast.

Separate zones for cooking and eating, living and sleeping were created by removing partitions or walls to provide larger, light-filled spaces. French doors were added to take advantage of the northerly aspect and to allow sunlight to stream through the rooms. The Baltic pine floors were sanded and coated with a polyurethane finish, and striped Finnish birch mats laid in strategic areas. Practical elements of country living were incorporated into the design. For example, spaces were specially made so that logs could be stacked on either side of the fireplace. Above the log-storage area are bookcases that reach the ceiling.

The mix of classic modern furniture and simple country pieces contributes to the charm of the interior and its feeling of refined comfort. Existing furniture was fitted with loose covers in cotton duck, which fit the cottage atmosphere perfectly. Modern accents include a table with painted blue steel legs in the dining room, and Philippe Starck's Miss Sissi lamps. Cassina dining chairs by Magistretti provide a blissful comfort level for long, happy meals in the kitchen. The owner's collection of contemporary art adds to the overall eclectic mix.

PREVIOUS PAGE *This sitting room was initially two rooms. French windows opening onto a verandah were added, and the oversized comfortable furniture covered with loose covers in cotton duck. The Baltic pine floors exude warmth.*

35

Sitting right on the edge of the lake, the design of the house is strongly influenced by subtle changes in light and wind. General living alters according to mood and weather; lunch may be on the front verandah one day and in the kitchen the next.

ABOVE *Rolled-down matchstick blinds give the enclosed verandah a soft, diffused light.* OVERLEAF
*This cane chaise is an example of early Australian country furniture. The sun-bleached finish and faded
striped cushions blend well with the painted verandah floorboards.*

40

The original dado line and tongue-and-groove boarding were retained along the entry hall and painted in the same colour as the lake. Magistretti chairs with rush seats have been set on striped Finnish birch matting. A Miss Sissi lamp adds a spot of colour.

Another of Philippe Starck's Miss Sissi lights perches on an early Australian pine cabinet containing a collection of miniature chairs.

42

OPPOSITE *A late eighteenth-century dresser in its original colour provides considerable storage for a collection of modern and old Italian china. The faded washed-out colour is in direct contrast with the colour of a modern table. The Cassina dining chairs are by Vico Magistretti.* ABOVE *The Lloyd Loom wicker chair sits well with a Persian rug of softly faded colours. Farmhouse pieces such as the sideboard can be found in antique and second-hand stores.* OVERLEAF *The fireplace in the sitting room has been surrounded by shelving for books and space for logs, which are neatly stacked in the Finnish style. The painting is by Sarah Faulkner.*

46

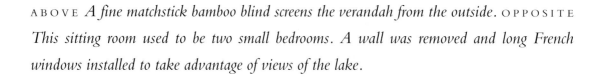

ABOVE *A fine matchstick bamboo blind screens the verandah from the outside.* OPPOSITE *This sitting room used to be two small bedrooms. A wall was removed and long French windows installed to take advantage of views of the lake.*

the lake house

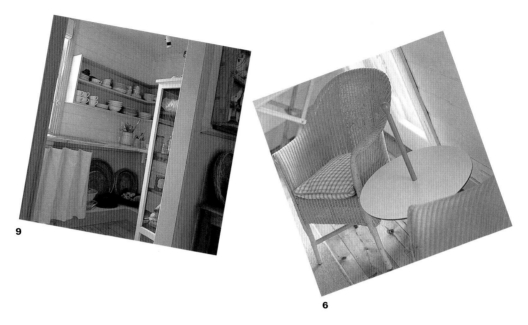

9

6

1 A special landscape deserves special treatment. Light and colour is more variable than in the city, and changes according to the landscape. If possible, live for a period of time in the space before making changes, so that you can incorporate specific needs into your design. Make a considered judgement of what is worth keeping and what is not. Keep initial purchases to a minimum until you complete all the details of your design. **2** Country living is very different to city living, and is better if kept simple and basic. Draw up a list of spaces required and plan accordingly. Prepare furniture layouts, and list existing furniture that is suitable and new items to be purchased. Furniture needs to comfortable, solid, practical and wear well. **3** It's much easier to form a coherent picture of what is required once the rooms are opened up and new windows and doors installed. Decide on finishes to the floor, which, in the country, should relate to the exterior paving. Sand and polish the existing timber floors if they are in good condition, and add atmosphere with rugs. Sisal matting is a pleasing alternative to carpeting. There are new wool carpets available which simulate the textures of this matting. **4** Blend the exterior paint colours with the landscape. Carry this theme throughout the interior in softer colours. Pale creams, grey greens, sparkling blues, off-whites, silver greys, pale soft aquas, deep blues, and brilliant yellows work particularly well. **5** Wherever possible, work with existing materials and finishes you like, but they should complement the character of the house. Endeavour to retain the character of the building. Sometimes patching up an old wall or applying a new coat of paint will breathe new life into a space. **6** Look for simple pieces of furniture that will add character to, and blend in with, the surrounding countryside. **7** Think texture and practicality when it comes to furnishing fabrics, for example, crisp white

do it yourself

12

1

4

cottons for bed linen, doonas rather than bedspreads, and large continental pillows on beds for comfort. Warm woollen or cashmere rugs will be appreciated on chilly nights. Large bedside tables are useful for holding books and other paraphernalia. **8** Relate window treatments to the character of the house. Simply gathered full-length curtains or roman blinds in plain natural cotton or linen work well. Try to relate the window treatment to the furniture—in this case, we used loose covers in cotton duck to cover the sitting-room furniture. **9** Choose the best of old and new, and blend the two. Mix patterns in china, glassware, cutlery and even furniture. **10** Country kitchens are the hub of the house. Have a large pantry to store excess fruit, vegetables, jams and preserves, and large preparation areas so that many people can work together at the same time. A large serving area is ideal for communal eating. Choose a stove with a large oven or preferably a double oven. Use timber, stainless steel or Carrara marble on benchtops. **11** Dressers are ideal for storing and displaying china. Drawers, bins and early Australian meat safes provide excellent capacity for storage. **12** Open shelving allows for easy access. **13** Outdoor awnings, matchstick blinds and large canvas market umbrellas are inexpensive to purchase and provide shade for verandahs and gardens. Decide if portability is an issue. **14** Effective and economical heating is essential in the country. Open fires can be augmented with gas or electric hydronic heating. **15** Think of the verandah as an extension of the house. French doors that open out to a verandah filled with wicker chaises with striped cotton fabrics, light and portable furniture finished in environmental colours, and stacked logs add to the casual feel of the house.

the clock

with any

success

the

def

tower

IN ITS ORIGINAL STATE, this space was the garage of a major industrialist. The ground floor was used to accommodate four vintage Rolls Royces and petrol bowsers, and the upstairs provided living quarters for the chauffeur.

The new owner understood the full potential of the house and was happy to retain elements of its original usage, such as the garage doors—which now act as a divider between the kitchen and dining areas—and the tiled floors, which still bear, in places, the imprints of cars and petrol bowsers. These aged features have added considerable interest and a sense of industrial history to the updated—but understated—interiors.

The semi-industrial touch was carried throughout the house in the renovation, softened here and there by judicious use of the existing collection of furniture and artwork. Colouring was limited to a warm white with pale grey surrounds, and applied to the French doors and balustrade. The exterior was painted to blend in with the slate roof and formal garden. The colours of the furnishings and finishes were kept neutral. The house maintains a refreshing simplicity that is in keeping with its history.

In the bedroom an American cherrywood veneer screen was used as a bedhead. Behind it, a walk-through dressing room replaced old-fashioned built-in cupboards.

A new bathroom was installed, which made use of the existing bath and basin. The new tiling reflected the overall integrity of the interior.

Natural materials were used as floor treatments with subtle changes in texture to reinforce the function of the room—sisal matting in the family room; pure wool carpeting in a herringbone pattern in the entry hall and on the stairs; jarrah flooring upstairs. Windows were covered with curtains or blinds made from sheer Irish linen.

In keeping with the industrial theme, corrugated acrylic-screen wall lights were used in conjunction with the downlights in the sitting and family rooms, and free-standing Constanza lights were added for practical and mood lighting.

OVERLEAF *Sheer linen curtains of the palest blue are simply hung in the bedroom. The floors are of rich jarrah, a pleasant foil for the Manilla chair.*

55

ABOVE *A veneered cherrywood bedhead draws your eye to its lustrous finish. Behind is the walk-in dressing room. The ceiling was allowed to run through to show off its intricate strapping, and the existing fireplace was sanded back and oiled. The result is a discreet elegance.* OPPOSITE *The dressing room features open full-length and double hanging rails, and drawers.*

With renovations, it is important to recognise the existing elements that will add character and can be incorporated into the new scheme. Too often, architects and designers impose their own idiosyncratic ideas on a renovation, and destroy precious and original material which cannot be replicated. Such an approach can also be expensive. By contrast, it is frequently possible to incorporate original design elements into the renovation, which has the advantage of helping with the budget as well.

In this case, the original flooring was maintained even though some of the tiles were cracked. The tiling and its layout was of such quality—and harked back to the house's industrial history—that it was considered of greater importance than an immaculate finish.

The garage doors were left intact as a room divider between the dining room and kitchen. The only alteration was to change the glass to an industrial quality.

The backs of the doors were lined with shelves for kitchen bowls, plates and baskets, softening the factory-like quality of the kitchen area and adding a practical dimension. The kitchen benchtops are of concrete with exposed aggregate edges.

OPPOSITE *The existing bath and basin were retained in the bathroom, and crisp, off-white square tiles added. A well-fitted mirrored cabinet takes up the length of a wall. The floors are of jarrah.*

ABOVE *A similar colour palette has been used on the walls and furniture, with interest and colour impact coming from rugs, books, paintings and antiques.* OPPOSITE *The garage doors that have remained in situ are a reminder of the building's history. The original dark finish of the staircase has been painted in toning colours to brighten up the room.*

PREVIOUS PAGES *B & B Italia settees and chairs covered in a cream cotton ottoman fabric sit on two sisal rugs bound with French braid. A Japanese door table holds books and ceramic ware. Floor-to-ceiling roller blinds in fine cane offer a tantalising glimpse to the garden beyond and screen some of the afternoon glare.* ABOVE *The original tiling and cupboard faces are unchanged, as with the flooring. Updates include a modern Ilve stove and sealed concrete benchtops with exposed aggregate edges.* OPPOSITE *The simplicity of the bedside table is complemented by the spare lines of the Constanza lamp.*

the clock tower

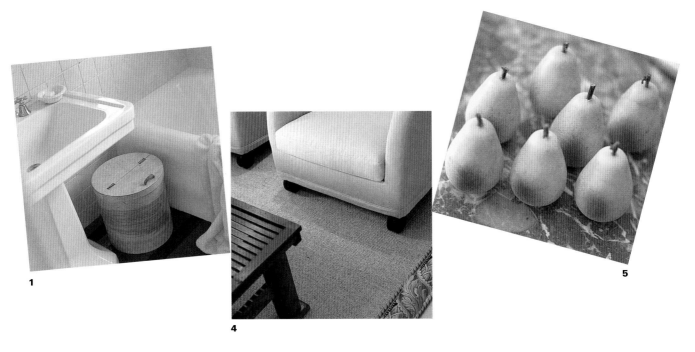

1

4

5

1 With any renovation, success lies in the detailing. Elements of the past that are important ought to be kept and worked into the modern structure. Although the space has an industrial demeanour, the result is friendly, and conducive to living. **2** Look at any existing space laterally. It may function as it is with minor adjustments. **3** It is particularly important that the texture and impact of the finishes complement each other. In this case, the original jarrah flooring and tiling were retained, concrete benchtops added in the kitchen, and veneered cherrywood used as a headboard in the bedroom. These 'hard' planes were married with soft, sheer linen window treatments, furniture covered in natural cotton, pure wool carpets in a herringbone design, and sisal matting in the bedroom and living room. **4** Use neutral colours that will complement the clean lines, and use details to produce effect. For example, the sisal matting underfoot has been bordered with an intricate

do it yourself

10

3

French braid, throwing into greater relief the deep cream B & B Italia furniture. **5** Artwork, sculpture, ceramics and furniture have been used to brighten up the neutral shell of the house. **6** Decide if you want an open or closed walk-in robe. An open-shelf hanging system requires a certain measure of neatness. **7** Consider lighting requirements—use a blend of uplights, downlights and occasional lamps for practicality and effect. **8** Tie in the choice of kitchen equipment with the general tone of the renovation. **9** Maintain the theme through to the selection of door furniture, bathroom towel rails and accessories, tapware, electrical switch plates and power points. **10** Views of the garden through door or window openings may act as a piece of artwork.

freedom

the beac

house

STEP THROUGH THE TURQUOISE front doors of this beach house and be treated to uninterrupted views of the horizon. You can sense the changes in each layer of landscape as your eye moves across the floor to the terrace to the simple formal garden that extends to the cliff edge, on to the sea and the sky.

This family holiday house is the epitome of space and light, situated on a magnificent cliff-top site that looks to the north over a seemingly endless sheltered bay. Taking inspiration from the setting, the colours of the sand and sea were brought indoors— the brilliant blues, blue-greens, whites and clear yellows—and thoughtfully expressed through a range of surface textures and furnishings. Though beach houses and the sea are usually associated with summer—blue seas that reflect clear, bright skies—we also took into account the seascape's grey, stormy and cold face when planning.

The house and its interior cater for the seasonal changes both visually and practically. The spaces are marvellous to live in, well organised and in harmony with the exterior architecture.

The interior is the result of thoughtful planning and detailing of joinery items. Three-dimensional stucco Venezia walls of the palest yellow tie the space together, punctuated in places by Flos Papillona uplights. A relaxed combination of modern and antique Italian furniture collapses the boundaries between the structural formality of the house and the casual style of living. On the whole, the design has been kept simple, the lines clean and minimal, and the finishes easily maintained. The overall quality of the house was not compromised in any way.

Windows capture and frame the various garden views. From one, you might see clipped hedges of sweet-smelling lavender; from another, a copper fountain by Peter Cole against a stark white exterior wall, pencil pines, old cypresses and a wide sweep of grass.

Such a serene environment defies competition, so we chose to work with the finest handcrafted natural materials and kept the detailing pure and elegant.

OVERLEAF *Large Italian hand-made terracotta tiles are a practical flooring finish in the sitting and dining rooms. A modern Italian dining table and chairs blend successfully with the oversized ceramic bowl by Bern Emmerichs that depicts family events.*

ABOVE LEFT *Entry to the house is through brilliant turquoise doors. The colour is picked up in the modern rug designed by Adam Rish, inspired by an Iranian kilim.* ABOVE RIGHT *The entry hall features hand-made terracotta Italian tiles, some of them bearing tiny dog paw prints. Vibrant colours are used throughout the house. The furniture is a deliberate mix of modern and early Italian.* OPPOSITE *A ceramic artist was commissioned to add a sensual finish to surfaces in the kitchen and bathroom, and the floors.*

80   *The shutters in the family room echo the turquoise doors from the entrance hall, the colour picked up again in the hand-made brilliant turquoise rag rug. The couch converts into a bed, and the Fiam table was chosen for its durability.*

A painting by Davida Allen hangs above an   83
early piece of Italian furniture. Other pieces
include Sity furniture and a Kick table.

B & B Italia Sity seating in the main sitting room is covered in a practical geometric design. The form of the unit is upholstered in a plain material to emphasise its simple elegance. An armoire holds the television and stereo equipment.

Arne Jacobsen chairs, beautifully comfortable and classical, are used in the family area.

The stucco Venezia wall treatment is used 87 throughout the house. An elegant French settee in walnut and ebony with a cane seat is set below a group of Australian Aboriginal paintings from Fitzroy Crossing.

ABOVE LEFT *A discriminating furniture mix that works. The Wink chair is covered in a bright yellow fabric with one green ear and a Le Corbusier table with pale blue legs is used as a desk. The ash book shelves are by Vico Magistretti.* ABOVE RIGHT *The spare lines of the queen-sized bed and doona box by Peter Sands rely on the straight-grain silver ash timber for impact. The duckboarding gives a maritime feeling. Bed covers have been kept fresh and pristine. A bright blue bolster makes reading in bed easier as well as providing a splash of colour. A cotton netting keeps away the mosquitoes.*

ABOVE LEFT *Timber-veneered vanity cupboards in one of the bathrooms were stained a pale turquoise to give the feeling of the water and topped with pure white Thassos marble finished with a rolled edge.*
ABOVE RIGHT *Ceramic mosaics by Bern Emmerichs add a decorative element around the basin.*

the beach house

8

13

1 Life near the beach is simpler and this lack of formality should be considered in every decision made. It's also a good opportunity for a bit of fun and personal light-hearted touches. **2** If you have a superb view, make this the major focus and keep the other colours and finishes to a minimum so they do not distract or compete. If you have little view, turn the property in on itself and give it a special scheme to relate it to the seaside environment. Juxtapose the indoors and outdoors. **3** Space is important, as is the freedom to move easily from indoors to outdoors, from the living to cooking area, bedroom to bathroom, and the opportunity to shift from indoor to outdoor eating. Space will also allow for big comfortable seating and easy dining for any number of guests. **4** An intermediary space such as a terrace with a hard surface is easy to maintain, and will help to reduce the amount of dirt tracked indoors. Large shade umbrellas or pergolas are ideal for shade control. Use a mix of casual furniture such as hammocks, lounges, and deck chairs with cotton and canvas covers. Plantings around the house provide a sense of privacy and act as a buffer from the sun and wind. **5** An outdoor cooking facility is handy for summer meals. Choose a site that is easily accessed from the kitchen and sitting room,

do it yourself

11

3

7

and make sure there is adequate seating. **6** Natural materials such as cotton, canvas, sisal, bamboo, timber and stone all have an affinity with the beach. Their practicality and versatility will leave you with more time to do things other than clean up! It is especially important for floors to be resistant to sand and dirt. **7** Use harmonious and restful colours throughout the house. **8** Furnishing materials can be mixed and matched— here's an opportunity to use a melange of checks, stripes and plaids. Unstructured furniture helps to create a light and airy feeling. **9** If privacy is not a problem, keep the windows unadorned. Otherwise, use bamboo, cane or rattan shutters or light cotton curtains. **10** Mix the unexpected—perhaps a primitive sculpture with a streamlined beach chair. **11** A generous-sized dining area close to the kitchen is invaluable. The kitchen and dining areas should be easily adaptable for large numbers or unexpected guests. Choose simple, comfortable furniture. **12** Make sure there is sufficient lighting. Create pools of light with standard and table lamps. **13** Too many paintings or artworks may detract from the view, so keep them to a minimum. **14** Wicker or bamboo baskets are useful for storage.

city apar

ment

SITUATED IN A GRACIOUS old suburb within a kilometre of the city, this apartment offers the convenience of easy access to urban attractions without sacrificing the space and greenery to which the owners were accustomed in their previous family house. The apartment building was designed in the sixties by a distinguished architect, and overlooks a magnificent public garden with the city skyline beyond.

There is a fundamental difference between an apartment in a large block and a self-contained dwelling—the foyers of large apartment blocks often tend to look rather faceless and cool. It is therefore important that the entrance hall to the apartment be inviting and homely, so that anyone stepping through the front door immediately feels welcome and at ease.

It is rare for apartment interiors to appeal to all the owners in the block. So, while sound in concept, we felt that the design of this particular apartment was slightly out of step with the demands and rigours of contemporary life—storage areas were limited, and there were space restrictions. The challenge was to create both real and illusory space by deploying materials and finishes with sensitivity.

A fresh pale green–blue paint inspired by the adjacent gardens was used throughout the apartment to create continuity. A slightly deeper green–blue carpet reflected the colour scheme that was chosen. The result is a simple space in which a much-loved collection of art, books and ceramics is shown to maximum advantage.

Curtains, which would have intruded on valuable wall and glass space and detracted from the view, were rejected in favour of slim-line venetians. The slats create interesting light patterns at various times of the day, reminding the owners of the outside elements even though they are in a high-rise building.

Built-in timber shelves serve as a sideboard in the dining room, and are used to hold books and ornaments in the living room. A built-in desk helps to reduce the need for loose furniture and keeps clutter to a minimum.

To create an illusion of space, a mirror was strategically placed in the dining area to bring the view of the 150-year-old botanical gardens into the apartment. Unlike a large painting, which could be used to the same effect, the mirrored view is constantly changing, with different intensities of light and colour at various times of the day and year.

OVERLEAF LEFT *The mix of old and new furniture, including the beautifully tactile pieces by Alvar Aalto, create a friendly, comfortable atmosphere.* OVERLEAF RIGHT *Adjustable timber shelving is used to hold a much-loved collection of objects and books collected during many travels. On the wall is an Aboriginal dot painting.*

On the book spines:

IC ROSES

Vincent van Gogh LETTERS FROM PROVENCE

DUTCH BY DESIGN

BABAR

INDIAN BASKETS OF NORTH AMERICA

BONNARD

Vanessa Bell's Family Album

DRAWING AND PAINTING THE PORTRAIT

FRANK WHITFORD Expressionist Portraits

modern primitives

CEZANNE and his art Nicholas Wadley

A GARDENER'S DIARY JOAN LAW-SMITH

ARTISTS' GARDENS

MATISSE PAINTINGS AND SCULPTURES IN SOVIET MUSEUMS

Working with the principle that if something functions well, why change it, the understated original white bathroom and kitchen have been retained. Some commercial brackets were added to house the timber shelving in the kitchen. A small laundry was installed.

While the interior of the apartment has been highly designed and each detail carefully considered, the overall effect is not one of imposed design. The living space is an expression of the owners' personalities; it is functional, very habitable, and a highly personal set of spaces.

OPPOSITE *Light, colour, careful placement of highly regarded objects, together with specially selected modern pieces have combined to create a unified interior.* ABOVE *Built-in shelving in the dining room holds fine china.* OVERLEAF *Saving the apartment from a sense of enclosure is the tiled north-facing terrace, which serves as an outdoor living–dining room. The size of a small room, it captures the winter sun and summer shade, and includes a culinary and perfume garden. It contains, in tubs and pots, an assortment of herbs and geraniums for the kitchen and two standard kumquats. A dining table comes in handy for* al fresco *meals.*

OPPOSITE *A magnificent city view is the backdrop to the botanical gardens.*

city apartment

10

6

1 In a block of apartments where all the finishes and spaces are similar, it is essential to personalise the space. The entrance hall to the apartment sets the feeling of the interior, and should be welcoming, and provide immediate insight into the people living there. **2** Apartments can be treated in many different ways but once you have decided on your own particular path, follow it through. Whatever you choose, be consistent. Have at least one wonderful room or an area with a sense of space. **3** An apartment usually lacks the intimacy of a house, so keep this in mind when selecting initial finishes. They should be friendly, practical and finely detailed. **4** Finishes and colours should be kept to a minimum. This itself will impart a feeling of space. Give architraves, skirting boards and walls the same finish throughout. **5** If the space is small, use floor-to-ceiling mirrors to create an illusion of space. **6** A sense of well-being can be easily achieved in a number of ways— good lighting, fresh flowers, inviting furniture or a richly patterned rug—something that attracts the eye. Upholstery fabrics of varying textures and weights are important for layering. **7** When selecting furniture, think comfort and practicality. The main furniture items are best kept simple and of a classical disposition. **8** Natural materials look best—cotton ottomans, small geometric-patterned wools, brightly coloured silks, leather and canvas. **9** Keep wall and floor tiles in the bathroom of the same size and colour. Remember to use non-slip tiles for the floors. White always looks fresh and clean, and coordinates easily. **10** Storage in apartments is generally inadequate and needs to be considered in detail. The easiest way to approach this

do it yourself

11

17

12

problem is to make exhaustive lists of what you need. Supplement built-in storage with free-standing items. The simpler the detailing of built-in storage, the better it looks. **11** To enhance the spaciousness of a small bedroom, tie in the decorative elements used. The pale blue-and-white quilt complements the fabric of the chair. The handcraft quality of the quilt is also picked up in the framed samplers hanging on the walls. **12** Augment the existing lighting with a detailed lighting layout closely related to the furniture plan. Add task and mood lighting. Modern French and Italian articulated fittings are designed to give more varied light, and their elegant styling adds definition to a space. **13** Where possible, the exterior view should be unimpeded. Curtains or blinds are an extension of the walls and should be specifically selected to provide suitable light control. Consider natural materials—timber venetians, sheer linens, cotton blinds, canvas awnings, and finely detailed roman shades. **14** Outdoor areas should be treated as an extension of the indoor space. They are valuable adjuncts to apartment living and, where possible, should act as an extra dining space or at least provide sufficient casual outdoor seating. **15** The colour of outdoor paving should coordinate with the colour of the interior flooring. **16** Terraces are of utmost importance for that glimpse of green. Well-pruned plants, colours and fragrances are all important considerations. **17** Simple and finely detailed open shelving allows easy access to everyday items.

the weath

important

the coun

needs of

itself a

is all

and the

try house

the land

priority

WALNUT TREE FARM IS A PICTURE of rural simplicity, and a haven created for loosening up and relaxing. Like many farms in the country, it consists of a main house and a series of sheds. The timber and corrugated iron structures massed around the garden area impart a satisfying architectural quality to the whole complex, immediately suggesting a renovation into a series of detached buildings, as in the old farming communities.

Farmhouse living has its quirks. The weather is all important, and the needs of the land itself are a priority. There is, in Australia, a historical preference for the European style of farmhouses and shedding, all of which work together to form a village. These simple forms and the honest use of materials have been modified for the Australian countryside; the result is a wealth of traditional solutions incorporated by today's architects and designers in a modern context, and an instinctive style that is unsurpassed.

The original house had little connection between indoors and outdoors. The first step was to employ a local builder to add a wide verandah, large enough for outdoor entertaining, around three sides of the house. This verandah was connected with timber decking to the existing garage, which was converted to extra sleeping accommodation and an en-suite bathroom. The result was a large enough space for outdoor living. Existing windows were converted to French doors, allowing every room to open directly onto the garden or the verandah.

Country living requires space, and so the next step was to turn three pokey rooms into one large room for cooking, eating and living.

The special quality of light in northern Victoria guided the choice of the colour scheme for the exterior of the old farm house and the surrounding buildings. The timber boarding is painted in the blue–grey of the eucalypts, and the roof of the main building, and roofs and walls of the farm buildings in a deep pink.

OVERLEAF *The perfumed climbing rose 'Devonensis', the colour of pale magnolia, seduces friends and family through the lattice arches.*

OPPOSITE *The informal entrance to the house is through a profusion of cottage planting that has been allowed to spill over the path. Plants were selected for their varying textures, colour compatibility with the landscape and suitability for the rigours of the climate.* ABOVE *A sculpture by Peter Cole is set in strong relief against the deep-pink corrugated iron walls of the hay-shed.*

The interior of this country house was designed to soothe, and imparts a feeling of great peace. It draws its inspiration from the surrounding countryside, building on what's good and adding new things.

A subdued eucalyptus blue–grey was used throughout the interior of the house. The horizontal boarding on the walls was retained and painted in this colour as a background for the paintings and furniture.

The mix of textures is a subtle and effective way of adding interest. The upholstered furniture was covered in a timeless William Morris design of blue–green leaves moving across a background the colour of a paper bag. All the blinds are of fine-crushed white linen.

The original Baltic pine floors were given a new lease of life. An assortment of kilims and coarse Belgian sisal rugs, selected for their subtle texture, durability and practical colouring, sit on the polished boards.

A dividing wall between two rooms was removed to create the main living space, which is now a combined kitchen, dining and sitting room—a large, pleasant and inviting area.

OPPOSITE *A simple timber gate made by a local craftsman leads through to one of the haysheds. An old pepper tree provides welcome shade in the summer months.*

OPPOSITE, CLOCKWISE FROM TOP LEFT *An early chair with an Emmet quality for leisurely swinging on the verandah. A skylight has been installed on the verandah roof to let more light into the house. Climbing 'Milk-maid' roses add a touch of romance. The barbecue area directly adjacent to the kitchen was built with old handmade bricks. Furniture on the verandah is deliberately unmatched, the common denominator being skilled craftsmanship. An elegant Italian Zanotta garden seat is mixed with a traditional wicker couch (this page). A planting of cerise poppies and lavender beside the pond.*

French doors opening straight onto the timber decking juxtapose the indoors and outdoors. A big comfortable easy chair is covered in a thirties William Morris print.

ABOVE LEFT *The interior boarding was painted a paler version of the exterior eucalyptus blue–grey.*
ABOVE RIGHT *A strong textural contrast: a fine William Morris print on armchairs and Belgian sisal matting.* OVERLEAF *The combined living and dining area features a long narrow wooden table and a matched set of original bentwood chairs. An early Tasmanian huon pine dresser holds a mix of antique and modern china.*

PREVIOUS PAGES *The French doors in one of the bedrooms open to a view of the pond. On the bed are a striped Marimekko doona cover and cashmere rug.* OPPOSITE *A new bathroom has been installed and panelled in Laminex lamipanel with shadow-line joints, a practical finish for the country. A European beech frame with laminate shelving surrounds the pedestal basin. Shaker boxes hold bathroom bits and pieces and simple rods act as towel rails. The deep bath is of cast iron.*

the country house

17

6

1

1 Consider the affinity of the house with the landscape—if possible, hold off making adjustments until you have been through four seasons on site so that you know exactly what you need to cope with the climatic changes. **2** Landscaping is as important as the structural construction or change, and planning should be effected more or less simultaneously. If possible, start on the garden before the house. Trees may need to be planted as windbreaks or to frame views, and they take time to grow. Make the most of the existing trees on the property and get rid of extraneous material that is obstructive. Plan a vegetable garden. **3** Build with two views in mind—the immediate view and the larger view. **4** Plan for the house and garden to be on the same level, with an intermediate space of timber decking to join them together. This allows for lots of different areas for activities. **5** Use paint to tie in groups of buildings and rooms. **6** Modern sculpture can give an unexpected lift to the serene environment. **7** The kitchen is of vital importance to country living. Include plenty of storage spaces such as pantries—food and hospitality are very important in the country. Have a good preparation area

do it yourself

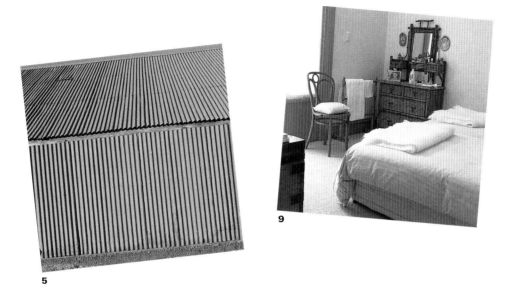

5

9

and bench space. **8** Keep the dining area close to the kitchen for ease of access. Comfortable chairs and a solid table are important for long meals. Make allowances for guests by having on hand fold-up seating. **9** Minimise the number of floor and wall finishes. If possible, select practical finishes such as sisal, timber or tiles for floors instead of carpets. **10** Plan for open fireplaces with space for log storage nearby. Back up with auxiliary heating. **11** Lighting, especially of the exterior, is important. You'll need to light the driveway, garden and verandahs, and spot-light the outdoor eating and entertaining area. **12** Ensure that there is an area for hanging up gumboots, coats and hats. Allow for adequate laundry facilities. **13** There should be ample power points in colours that blend in with the paint. **14** Security is becoming increasingly important in isolated areas. **15** Install flywire on doors and windows. Keep window furnishings simple, or leave them bare. **16** Outdoor furniture needs to be in the right place. Ensure that there are lots of places to sit outside—in the garden, vegetable garden, and other places of interest. **17** Furniture should be portable, durable and comfortable.

131

the peri

the layers

and new

textures an

add a su

ng of old

of old

fabrics and

d house

patterns

yptuousness

GLIMMERS OF A ROMANTIC past flow through this family house, which was built in the scale and opulence typical of a bygone era. While it provided the perfect setting for a large collection of paintings, furniture and ceramics that has been handed down through generations, the Victorian grandeur and museum-quality furniture were hardly ideal for the contemporary needs of a growing family.

The challenge was to integrate modern elements with the old and the grand, create interiors that reconciled the needs of the children, and use the traditional elements of the house without being too precious. We worked with an architect to define the spaces.

The budget was generous, and the collection of furniture and decorative objects large enough to be culled in order to find the appropriate pieces for each setting.

Colour was used extensively and boldly. Fabric patterns and textiles were combined in unusual mixtures, and favourite paintings and furniture carefully incorporated into the design. Specially commissioned modern artworks were used for that element of surprise. In the formal entrance, for example, a hand-made fantasy chandelier with brilliantly coloured glass teardrops designed by Mark Douglass hangs over the grand balconied staircase.

A separate living area with an indoor pool, billiard table and computer room was designed to cater for the children's needs and avoid the wear and tear in the main house. It is spacious and light, and the colours complement the vibrant palette of the main house.

The choice of colours for the house began with the exterior scheme. The palette was based on traditional heritage colours, but these were made stronger as the scale of the house and the owners' love of colour allowed for a richness and depth not usually possible on a smaller scale.

Particular consideration of the needs, styles of living and personalities of the family, balanced with respect for the architectural character of the house itself has produced an interior that happily reconciles the traditional and the contemporary.

OVERLEAF *Handpainted gold stars on the raspberry walls and vivid stripes of the upholstery on the highback chairs add a light-hearted touch to the serious family furniture and paintings.*

137

PREVIOUS PAGES *Silk curtains with tiebacks in the dining room complement the striped silk upholstery of the modern dining chairs. As a boy the owner loved the richness and redness of the dining room. The colour was retained, and gold stars painted on for a touch of whimsy. Other furniture in the room include Regency chairs and a commode.* OVERLEAF *The sitting room is exceptionally large and could have been intimidating if furnished as a single space. It was divided into three sections and decorated in colours picked out of a favourite painting from the Heidelberg school. Materials were specifically selected in pinks, turquoises and yellows, and cleverly detailed to create a richness of effect. Old and new fabrics, and textures and patterns were layered for a luscious finish. Oversized furniture was teamed with existing antique pieces. One of a matched pair of cedar bookcases displays a precious Limoges dinner service.*

OPPOSITE *In a side entrance, a triangular floor mosaic set into the terracotta tiles captures the family history, a witty and modern version of a coat of arms by ceramicist Bern Emmerichs.*

A completely new kitchen was installed. The cupboards are in cherrywood, and perfectly complement the rich red jarrah floors.

The large central trolley in the kitchen is set on castors and can be easily pulled to the serving area or sink.
The adjustable open shelving holds durable everyday china.

150

ABOVE *A detail of the en-suite bathroom showing a duckboard bench. The floor and walls are of marble.*
OPPOSITE *The bathroom was finished in marble tiles with a fine blue inset, and a colour-matched heated towel rail was installed. The bath is of cast iron.*

the period house

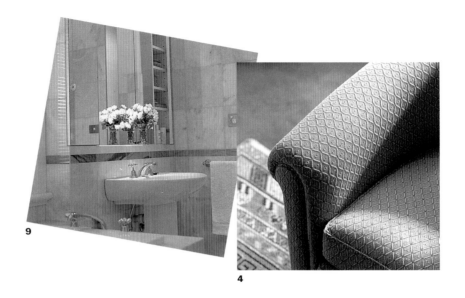

9

4

1 There are many ways to treat a period house—you can keep it authentic or use it as a shell for a modern interior, or a mix of both. Consider today's lifestyle needs and take into account how you wish to live. **2** The changes in the size and function of rooms have to be considered. Many old houses tend to be fairly unwieldy and need to be simplified. Make sure that the rooms are where you want them. **3** Use elements of the period house for today without getting too bogged down in history. Use the unexpected, and be brave—use strong bursts of colour to pick up the idiosyncrasies of the house and make them effective features. **4** Sumptuous colour, texture, and strong designs will hold their own in such a setting. Apply a multiplicity of finishes. **5** With furniture, balance the old with the new. Mix period elements and comfortable, modern pieces. Aim for an element of surprise. **6** Use more decorative and dramatic lighting. **7** The greater height of the ceiling

do it yourself

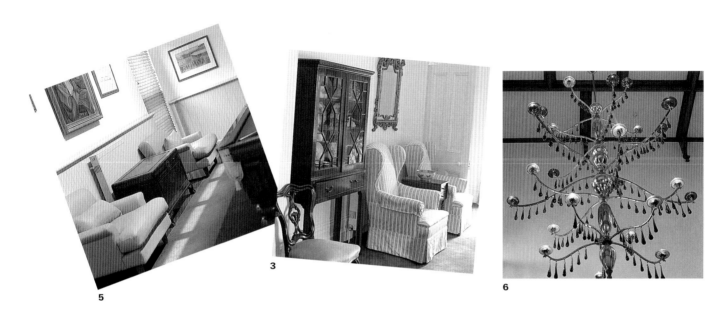

5

3

6

provides an ideal opportunity for wall fittings. **8** Choose either traditional or modern door furniture and be consistent throughout. Match with other fittings in the house. **9** Keep the lines of the bathroom simple and flowing. Use tiles of the same size for the floor and wall. Square tiles tend to work better than rectangles, and the larger the tiles, the less cutting they will require. **10** With a period house, consult architects and skilled tradespeople. Ask to see some of their work so that you know what kind of quality to expect. Get quotations from two or more parties for a comparison. It is imperative that you prepare the same briefs for each quotation detailing what you want. Ask for an itemised quote. **11** Consult a heating expert for advice on updating the heating.

living with

artworks

ART OFFERS US AN IMAGINATIVE experience. It extends our mental horizons and gives distinction and character to both interior and exterior spaces. Ideally, the inclusion of quality artworks should be an important consideration at the initial planning stage of any interior design project. If outside expertise is necessary, it should be involved at this stage.

There are, of course, many ways of approaching the placement of artworks. An entire room or landscaping project may be conceived around a particularly distinctive work. Walls and spaces may be nominated at the planning stage as being specific areas to showcase an existing or future collection.

Some people need help in selecting and placing artworks in either domestic or public settings. If you lack confidence, the designer and/or art consultant can gently guide you. Go regularly to exhibitions at the state gallery, serious commercial galleries and major auction houses. Search out successful examples of the placing and setting of artworks. Develop the courage to make brave decisions; uncertainty and tentativeness invariably result in mediocrity and compromise.

Strong contemporary minimalist design is often suitable for bold large-scale painting or sculpture, and can create a major focus within a space. Sometimes even changing the colour of a wall from beige to a vibrant colour can add additional drama to the artwork.

Art of quality need cost no more—indeed may sometimes cost less—than an inferior piece.

Good art is an investment.

PREVIOUS PAGES *Place artworks where they can be seen so that you can get pleasure from them all the time. This watercolour by John Olsen has been hung above the kitchen sink.*

OVERLEAF *An abstract painting by Paul Partos enhances the minimalist dining setting.*

PREVIOUS PAGES *The lines of the Magistretti Sinbad chair, with its leather cover based on the horse*   165

blanket, is a perfect foil for the three-dimensional work by Colin Lanceley that hangs on a panelled

European ash timber-veneered wall. OPPOSITE *Even with a small budget it is still possible to buy*

exciting high-quality artworks. If the amount allocated is generous and sufficient time is allowed for a

wide choice of prospective pieces to be considered, the desired result can be sensational. The sculpture is by

Antonio Colangelo; the painting by Yvonne Audette. OVERLEAF *Sunlight streams into this corner of*

a bedroom, accentuating the abstract by Brett Whiteley.

ABOVE *A wire sculpture by Antonio Colangelo.* OPPOSITE *A touch of whimsy lightens the formality of this garden, while its brilliant ceramic hues strengthen the depth of green in the background. The work is by Deborah Halpern.* OVERLEAF *The spareness of this painting by John Olsen accentuates the clean lines of the contemporary furniture.*

living with artworks

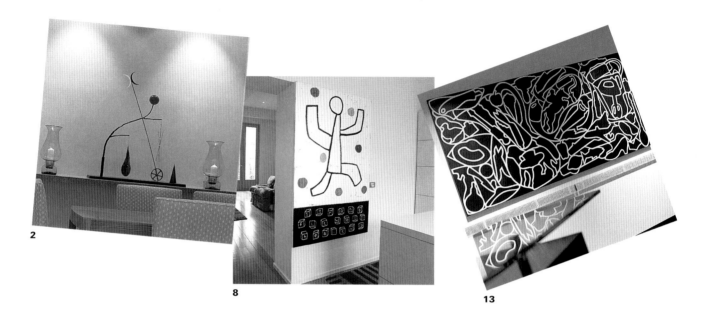

2

8

13

1 To learn about art, you need to appreciate its history, and to keep in touch with the contemporary art scene. Talk to artists and visit their studios. **2** Consider a wide variety of artists and craftspeople who can provide a strong degree of individuality. Don't limit yourself to just paintings—consider sculptures, ceramics, glass, metal work, textiles, and furniture. **3** Visit good commercial galleries and discuss artists' work with gallery directors. Familiarise yourself with work in national and state galleries. **4** There is a wealth of reviews in newspapers and magazines, and books by respected critics and authors on specific artists. **5** Take art appreciation courses. **6** There is a range of work available at reasonable prices. Young contemporary artists can be a sound investment for the future. **7** Well-known and established artists are usually in mid-career and more expensive. **8** Select paintings on their merit, and not as an accessory to decoration. They do not need to blend with the interior environment: an element of surprise can be exhilarating. **9** Lithographs, drawings and prints are a way of enjoying an artist's work at a reasonable price. When framed simply, they have a delicate quality. While they do not always supply the impact of major works, they nevertheless have a charm that requires a more measured appraisal. **10** Sculpture can be used to punctuate indoor and outdoor spaces. **11** Banks and institutions are investing in work by young artists. This way of starting a collection adds a very personal touch

do it yourself

17

18

to the interior of your house. **12** A collection of art need not be static. You can add to it, and re-sell items you are not as attracted to as you were initially. As you develop confidence, be bolder and braver. **13** Large-scale paintings look good in major spaces, while small works can be grouped together to form a cohesive whole. **14** As a rule, artefacts look better grouped together, rather than placed here and there. Television sets, pianos and stereo systems are best left unadorned. Leave some walls bare; not all walls require adornment. **15** Be selective—don't just hang it because you own it. **16** Hang paintings so that the centre of the work is at eye level. **17** Remember to plan early for artworks in your furniture and lighting layouts. Artworks should be always well lit and not in shadow. They are generally better lit from above. Picture lights attached to the frame detract from the work itself. **18** Good artworks are better hung in simple frames. A professional picture framer will assist in the selection of frame mount and size. Don't use non-reflective glass as it reduces the colour intensity and quality of the work. **19** Prepare a succinct brief when commissioning an artist. **20** Take artworks 'on approval' and try them in situ. Most galleries would be pleased to comply. Auction houses are worth frequenting and often have quite extraordinary bargains.

there are

gentle with

working w

times to be

no time to

times to be

colour and

th colour

brave, but

be dull

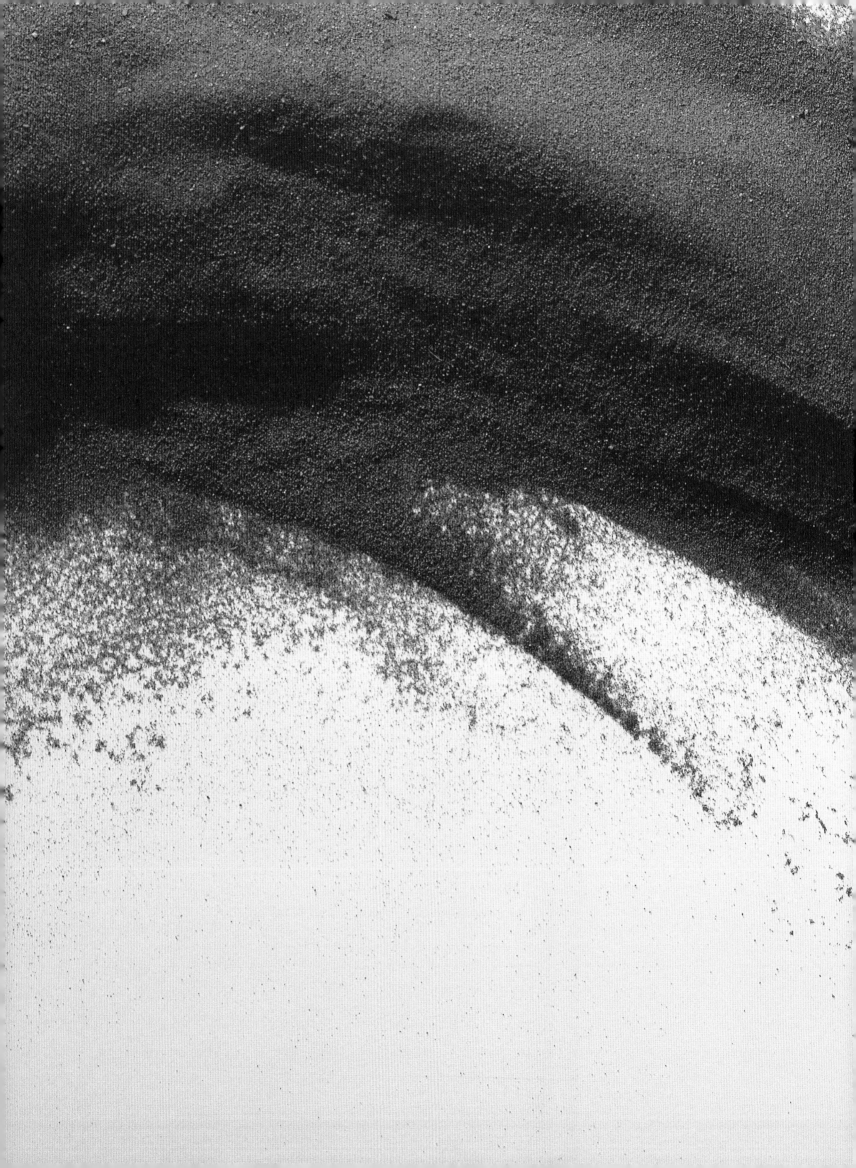

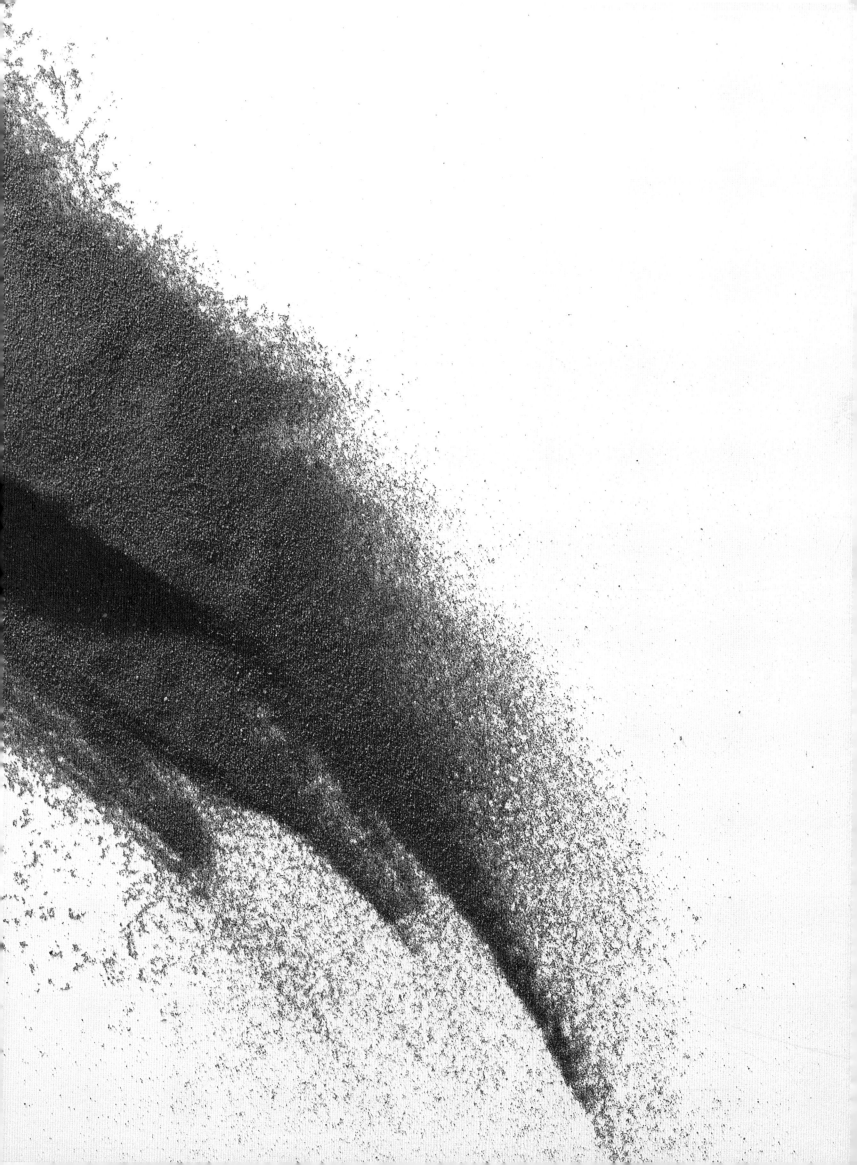

THE COLOUR WHEEL consists of three primary colours: red, yellow and blue. The three secondary colours are orange, green and violet, and tertiary colours such as turquoise are the result of mixing equal portions of a primary and a secondary colour.

While the colour wheel is a useful tool in helping us to understand colour effects, your imagination has no limits. We all know the objects we love. What is the intangible quality that we find attractive and immediately respond to? Besides structure and form, colour is probably a contributor to this special quality. Applied well, colour imparts an overall vibrancy, a touch of the unexpected and light-heartedness. It has the ability to transform a place or a person, to uplift and excite.

Picture the vitality of the buildings on the tiny secluded island of Burano, one of the most colourful sights on the Venetian lagoon. The residents take great pride in the façades of their dwellings, and the result is truly sensual and uplifting. Most of the paint is hand-made by the islanders, and applied in an unselfconscious manner. Nevertheless, strict rules apply—the façades must be regularly repainted because of the humidity, and the shades of colour used must remain constant. Boats in the harbour are treated with the same enthusiasm. The lesson we can take away from Burano is the islanders' joyous openness in the face of colour.

There are many ways of handling colour; the trick is to pick the one you feel most comfortable with. Colour that has been applied with abandon and a lack of self-consciousness is almost always recognisable. However, this is not to say that a studied and carefully planned colour palette is not a work of art! Apply colour with a distinctive quality that can be called your own. With the range available today, you can create different and individual moods.

Inspiration for colour palettes can come from anywhere. Even the way light creates change in a landscape can conjure up a whole new set of ideas.

Early artists such as Piero della Francesca (1420–1492) introduced colours such as ochre browns, distinctive blues and a particularly vital green that became fashionable throughout fifteenth-century Europe. Cubism in the beginning of the twentieth century developed a palette of grey, black and white which perfectly encapsulated this austere period.

In Matisse's vibrant coloured cut-outs, we experience strong blocks of clear colour—bright blue, scarlet, orange and ochre. This use of colour originally infuriated the Parisian critics, but his influence can now be seen in everyday objects throughout the world.

The Australian landscape provides us with a wonderfully varied palette. The natural environment contains every imaginable hue, from the bright reds of the desert interior to the golden wheat belt under vibrant blue skies, to the glowing yellows of the acacia, to the clear iridescent turquoise of tropical waters. In the cities, steel, glass, granite and marble interspersed with the familiar mish-mash of housing contain countless subtle and muted tones.

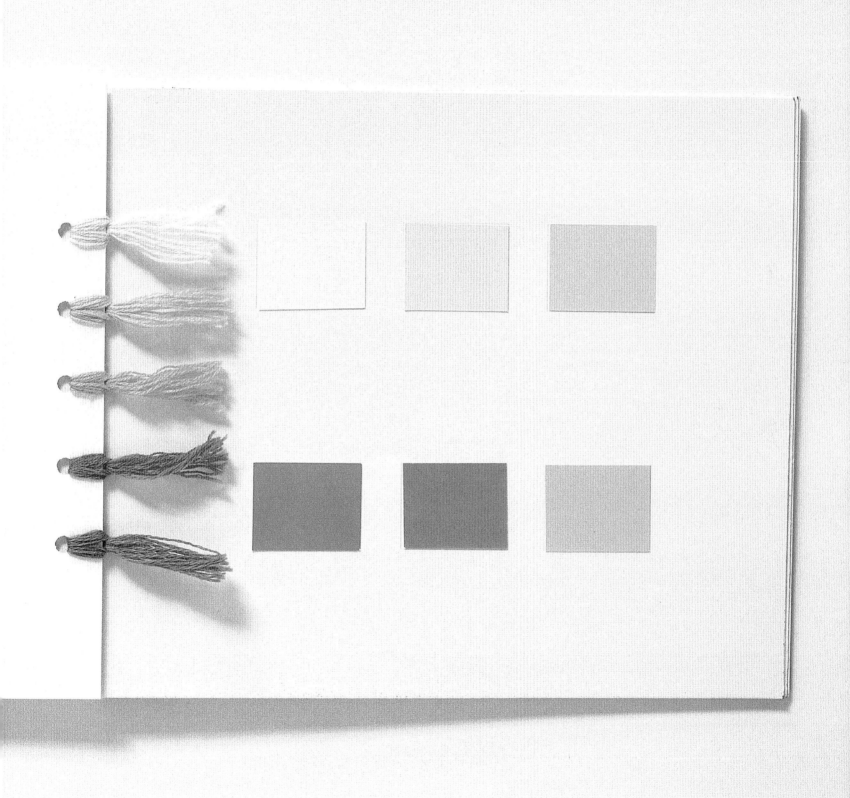

The intricacies of early textiles summon to mind wonderful subtle colour palettes. Flemish tapestries woven at the beginning of the sixteenth century, for instance, were dyed in forest tones of blue–greys, forest greens and pale yellows.

In his desire to move away from the gloom of Victorian interiors, where darkness was a sign of wealth, English artist William Morris from the Art and Crafts Movement revived a palette of light, clear colours in shades of bluish green, darkish green, soft pinks and deep cream, often against backgrounds the colour of a paper bag. These restrained colours mirrored those in nature, and were hugely appreciated and admired.

The French have dictated fashion in many aspects of our lives for centuries, and stimulated major movements in art and design. Colour applied with such a sense of sureness and style, and it is not surprising to see colour playing a considerable role in French architecture, churches and cathedrals, all of which were—and still are—lavishly decorated and gilded. This influence has continued till today in the enriched shop fronts and signage throughout the country. The French people use colour in a most refined and studied manner; this is evident in the tonal layering of colours and fabrics in French furnishings.

182

In Morocco, too, you can find an exotic mix of colour that is characteristic of its location at the intersection of the Mediterranean and the African continent. In souks, the open-air bazaars where everything happens, colour is everywhere: on the weaving looms of artisans who work in an amazing range of hues; in the range of fresh produce; and in the Moroccans' flamboyant robes of saffron, turquoise, lilac and tomato red—tantalising combinations of colours that are at once sophisticated and primitive.

And then there is nature, the simplest and most complex of stimulus. Nature provides a breadth of choice that takes us away from the safe, and often dull, everyday solutions. Select as many or as few colours as you need for the task to hand—do you want to create a mellow or vitalizing or fresh or uplifting or dynamic or serene environment?

Our design office is greatly influenced by the special qualities of the Australian landscape; our colour palette has evolved through working with clients across the continent and by responding to different environments in each state.

OPPOSITE *Coordinating colours for products being developed for the building industry by Nexus.*

From the centre of Australia, we have drawn on the colours of the extraordinary red soil and the local flora and fauna. By the sea, we are fascinated by the subtle changes of light, the water, the sky, and the sand, and use these colours with very slight nuances to reproduce the ever-changing seascape.

One of our favourite working palettes comes from the bush. The blue–greys of the gum leaves are a particularly kind indoor–outdoor colour. Add to this a mix of silver-grey bark and a deeper vital green, and the result is a satisfying colour scheme that is easy to live with.

Technology is making colour reproduction readily available. As consumers, this means the opportunity to choose from millions of different hues. What it does not do, however, is offer personal palettes to suit the individual.

Relate colour to the world you live in, and administer it with a sense of daring. The present trend of accurately matching historical colour schemes is fraught with danger. Pigments in the past were much more limited, and designers and architects of the day did not have such a wide variety of colours from which to choose. It is difficult to use a restricted heritage palette when all the colours in contemporary clothes and accessories are part of the extraordinary range now available. Modern life tends to make a historical palette appear dull and lifeless. Remember that you are not designing for fashion, but with an awareness of it.

The idea that certain colours are not to be used together has little or no relevance today, where anything is possible. Contemporary fashion looks particularly at home in modern minimalist rooms. Strength of colour, if applied with a sure hand, can transform an ordinary palette into a work of art. Shutters, doors and wrought-iron work, when picked out in sharp, contrasting colours, add interest and enliven both interiors and exteriors.

Our ideal house is a place of comfort, rest and enjoyment; a place to spend some of our most important times eating, sleeping, talking, reading and playing. Colour has a role to play in all of this, so whatever you do, be brave.

Finding a starting point for a colour scheme can be challenging. Technology has been a mixed blessing. On the one hand, books, magazines, film and television provide a plethora of instant and continually changing images of rooms and interiors; on the other, they can also confuse and intimidate us as we try to isolate ideas that might work for us. It takes years of working continually with colour to understand what works and what doesn't.

Draw inspiration from objects around you. It may be a view from the window, a mix of colours in a painting, a palette of natural colours derived from a swatch of fabric, or a group of colours that you feel comfortable with. At Nexus we often derive our palettes from the landscape and echo the colours in our interiors. A view of trees in the afternoon light may provide us with the interior colours for a country cottage. A sliver of a building glimpsed from a city window may suggest the colours for an urban apartment.

We may use a single colour with lighter and darker tones when working with a small house. In a larger house, where colour changes can add interest, we harmonise the colours so that there is continuity as the eye travels from room to room. Where rooms are not seen together, the colours should still be related.

Designers, like artists, have a readily discernible
style and palette. Although each design is built
around the needs of the client, common themes will
carry through their work. We always try to use
natural products such as cotton, timber and stone.

OPPOSITE *The blue wall is a brave choice against the brightly coloured painting, adding a vibrant feel* 189
to the room.

To maintain harmony and simplicity, where possible, have the colour scheme follow through from the exterior to the interior. For example, a house with a soft yellow lime-wash façade can have a cream interior scheme. A timber exterior stain can be repeated internally using a diluted version of the exterior stain. The quality of external light is also significant. In hotter climates, where the light is bright and strong, the palette tends to be high key. In cooler zones, the softer light usually calls for a more subtle effect.

Once you have selected the main background colour, develop the palette. Because the colour shell is restrained, it is relatively easy to introduce strong colours to add excitement. The interior palette should flow naturally from room to room, with each colour enhancing the next. Maintain a continuity of interest. Consider the proportions of the room, its function, the quality of light and personal colour preferences when developing colour combinations. Existing pieces of furniture and artworks may also dictate the strength and choice of colours. Light colours emphasise spaciousness. Neutrals are peaceful. Bright colours are exhilarating and inviting.

Many people lack confidence in handling colour and opt for a safe palette of beiges. The final result could very well be a let-down because it offers little or no stimulation. Our senses respond to colour just as they do to sound and taste, and they do not have to match exactly to be successful. There are times to be gentle with colour and times to be brave, but no time to be dull.

Don't approach the interior design and decoration of your house with anxiety. Think about what really matters to you, the type of environment that is likely to give you the greatest pleasure. Look carefully at what is around you. If you keep it simple, and integrate the changes you wish to make, the results will be pleasing.

OPPOSITE *Wattle-yellow walls are a good counterpoint for the coolness of the stainless-steel stove. The timber cupboards evoke memories of Australian meat safes.*

OPPOSITE *This bright purple cane chair with a provincial cotton fabric cushion makes an effective combination because it is so unexpected.*   197

Inside

This en-suite bathroom in an inner-city warehouse has been finished in Laminex Lamipanel. The result is easy to maintain, and the shadow-line joints provide a flash of sophistication.

1   The bathroom walls and the vanity unit have been panelled in Laminex Lamipanel 'Dune'.

2   The door has been painted in Dulux 'Silverlawn', satin enamel.

3   The wall have been painted in Dulux 'Coastlight', low-sheen acrylic.

198

1

2

3

Inside

The sage-green Laminex cupboards, cream walls and
Baltic pine floors still look fresh after twenty years'
wear and tear. The classic lines of this kitchen have
ensured its longevity, comfort and utility.

1   The door frame has been painted in Dulux 'Sea Lane',
satin enamel.

2   The walls have been painted in Dulux 'Custard
Cream', low-sheen acrylic.

3   The cupboards and one of the island benches have been
panelled in Laminex 'Cactus', texture finish.

Inside

The gentle curved forms of the kitchen cupboards and island bench are echoed throughout the apartment.

1 The ceiling has been painted in Dulux 'Shell White', low-sheen acrylic.

2 The bulkhead has been painted in Dulux 'Basic Beige', satin enamel.

3 All the cabinets have been panelled in Laminex laminate 'Paper Bark' with a flint finish.

1

2

3

working with colour

6

8

10

1 To begin a colour scheme, first take photographs of the surrounding landscape—whether it be in a suburb, in the city, or in the country. These photographs, when assembled alongside the paint colour chips, will assist you with colour selection. The surrounding landscape should have an influence on your initial thinking. **2** Consider the architectural style or period of the house, and the exterior finishes and materials proposed or existing for the roof, walls, window frames, exterior doors and paving. **3** Start by choosing colour for the largest area of the house. This colour is usually a subtle extension of the landscape. If it is a new house start with the roof, followed by the walls, and architectural components such as fascias, trims, guttering and window frames. Do the same for an existing house but be mindful of items that cannot be easily changed such as the existing roof tiles. **4** It is difficult to choose an exterior colour without doing colour samples. Paint the samples as large as you can on actual areas of the house and live with them over a period of time. Step across the road and look at your samples from a distance during different times of day and at night. **5** By now, the exterior colour palette should be formed. An occasional surprise such as a strong, clear colour on a particularly fine architectural detail can stimulate the senses, for example, a brilliant turquoise door on a white building. **6** Now select the interior colour palette. To maintain harmony and simplicity, we prefer, where possible, to have the colour scheme follow through from the exterior to the interior. Our usual method of working is to keep the interior colour very neutral. We regard the interior colour of the house as enhancing the exterior and as a background for the furnishings. **7** Consider individual preferences: colours that everyone living in the house will be happy with, colours they won't, rich colours, pale colours, neutrals, whites. **8** Some people have

do it yourself

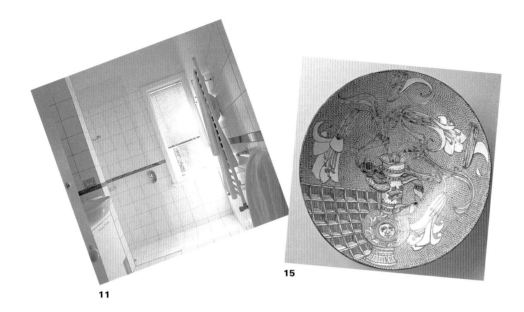

11

15

a tendency to want to use too many different colours, not understanding that you build on colour and that every addition has a bearing on the final result. A scheme that may appear dull initially will, in all possibility, end up being quite vibrant after the addition of people, paintings, books, rugs, and artefacts. We come back to the 'less is more' axiom, and aim for the simplicity of a restful, happy background. **9** Ensure that the palette flows from room to room, with each colour enriching the next. Choose a deeper shade of the shell colour for architectural elements like skirtings, architraves and window frames. This evokes a feeling of harmony and restraint, and shows a respect for the architecture of the building. **10** We prefer strong colours to come through in paintings, textiles and fabrics. However, there are no rules. We sometimes use very strong colour to add interest to a room with limited external views or, as in the case of a study, to add warmth and a feeling of comfort. **11** Keep bathrooms crisp and light. Walk into a bathroom with simple white tiles on floor and walls, a white bath and basin, good mirrors and you immediately feel cleansed. White also gives a sense of space. **12** Ceilings generally appear darker than walls, so we reduce the ceiling colour with 25 to 50 per cent white, depending on the colour and the degree of light in the room, so that it appears to be the same colour as the wall. Add a touch of amber or ochre to white to take the frost off the colour. **13** We generally use acrylic low-sheen for the walls and ceiling, an oil-based satin for skirtings, doors and window frames. **14** Colourful rooms can be inspired by a favourite painting, ceramic or artworks. **15** Finally, you must feel secure and comfortable with your choices.